MW01142328

CLINIC DAY

CLINIC
DAY

DIANA FITZGERALD BRYDEN

Brick Books

National Library of Canada Cataloguing in Publication

Bryden, Diana Fitzgerald
  Clinic day / Diana Fitzgerald Bryden.

Poems.
ISBN 1-894078-39-X

I. Title.

PS8553.R94C54 2004   C811'.6   C2004-903124-4

We acknowledge the Canada Council for the Arts, the
Government of Canada through the Book Publishing Industry
Development Program (BPIDP), and the Ontario Arts
Council for their support of our publishing program.

The cover and author photographs are by John Knechtel.

The book is set in Bembo and DIN Mittelschrift.

Design and layout by Alan Siu.

Printed by Sunville Printco Inc.

Brick Books
431 Boler Road, Box 20081
London, Ontario   N6K 4G6

brick.books@sympatico.ca

For Jerry Berg and Pier Bryden

Contents

AGE AND THE SECRETARY

CLINIC DAY

EXCAVATE

EPILOGUE

PROLOGUE

Open Letter

The early car's mine.
I leave before the day
puts hardware on;
ride east all the way.

I leave before the day
abandons slow calm.
Ride east all the way,
and now a storm

abandons slow calm.
We pass the bridge
and now a storm
has torn the sky's edge.

We pass the bridge.
Sharp, bleaching light
has torn the sky's edge,
cancelled night.

Sharp, bleaching light.
Freeway, sleepers, me.
Cancelled: night,
dreams, lullaby.

Freeway, sleepers. Me,
I turn the page to see
dreams, lullaby
move through the city.

I turn the pages. See
the early car: mine
move through the city,
all its hardware on.

MORNING

Current

The city belongs to animals. Rampant,
electric, wincing current.
Cockroaches with stiff brown backs,

night cats, pacing, thread
her dreams. Birds roam and feed,
ride the green and silver breeze.

A shudder ripples trees, green artery
that mines her spirit, binds it
to morning, evening; flesh

and blood. The day is dust:
paper, stairs and corridors.
Birds fly through her dream-vaults.

In the dark she leaves for work.
Small part in the play, its hushed
community of earners that starts

the day, closes off the night.
Thin slice of time, undefended.
There the hospital, its useful glow:

rows and banks of light, behind
which breath circulates or, in
squeaking, burning rooms, runs out.

Sleepers Awake

Sleepers rise, roll up
their bags, fold coats,
feed dogs. Leave offerings,

mark the gateway
to the garden: a pair
of plastic slippers,

daisy browning on
a broken strap, seen
by the secretary (pricked

by haste she doesn't stop).
North of the church, two men:
one with his back to her,

curved in his wheelchair.
A squirrel near his feet
turns a nut in finicky paws.

The autumn air thick
and warm. The younger man,
providing tension, pulls

the other's arm. Gently, loosens
the dishonoured limb, returns it
to its owner in a smooth, elastic

gesture. Takes the hand,
uncurls the fist, flexes
all its helpless fingers.

The body's still,
apart from this:
closed hand coaxed open

like a flower, a letter,
a window from its sill.
Like a bird's gold wing.

Sanctuary

Once the secretary's moved
she takes a different route
to work. This one leads her

straight to the heart:
St. George the Martyr.
He becomes her patron saint.

The courtyard's portal stands
alone, metal archway
freed by fire. Old church gone.

The garden's invitation:
lay your head down,
rest, or weep. Each

corner folds or opens, offers
entry or protection. Benches
dwell in sunlight; cloisters

shadow sleepers. Small birds eat.
Pedestals stand empty – beauty
of snapped columns. Quiet.

When she dreads re-entry
into the hospital's stacked furrow,
its highly-charged, pain-ridden flow,

she stops at this pastoral island,
stands at its edges and
steps in.

The singer needs a stage, sleepers
a stone passage – shelter
for the shelterless as they

survive the seamless days.
If she joined their progress
her material world, like theirs,

would blur. Her
self-appointed sanctuary
is shared by them – see

their shadows as they flee
the courtyard early in the day.
Exit sleepers, now awake.

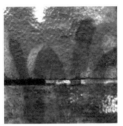

EVERY DAY

Work

On her way to work she
moves fast, with some urgency
disembarks from the streetcar, stops

for coffee. Taps her foot in line.
They, with different purpose
opposite the coffee-shop

observe the blind, swift progress
of the working world. (A world
that works, but not for them.)

She passes, running, coffee held aloft.
The sleepers watch, she watches them.
A dollar's tossed. The day's begun.

She arrives early, unlocks
white doors with her set
of bright gold keys – series

of unfolding cabinets.
Chatelaine of this mansion,
she feels the solid click

of turning slots. The quiet of
unpeopled hallways, tiles
the blurry cream of mushroom soup.

Eye Eye Eye

Industry, Intelligence, Integrity!
The city's sensible alternative
to revolutionary cry.

(See Soviet posters, workers'
chiselled forearms, fists airborne,
upraised, praising work itself.)

Equity, Respect, Harmony, Prosperity!

Every Day

Snowy streets. Whole clusters
of swaying, drooping men
drink from brown-

wrapped bottles. Women
stand alone. Cold legs
tremble in freezing air,

whole body wracked
in a stunned vibration, as if
attempting to remember

something simple and familiar.
Blake knows this stretch – narrow
splint that binds Queen Street

to naked lots and sleeping factories.
Library, fire-station, where stands
the random clutch of men;

diner where he warms himself –
first sets down his grateful mask.
Become a private man again

he's dreaming of Annapolis:
sent up to bed one summer night
a small boy eyes the miracle play

of light and shadow on his wall –
a frieze that shivers as the sun
slips through its net of leaves

and apple blossoms fall.
In spring the same boy, now a man
far from Annapolis, observes

a new, ironic miracle in the sunken
plaza of the Hydro mall.
He sells his papers on the street,

trembles at the sight: magnolia
– swift, fluorescent spasm.
Its eerie glow is green-tinged white.

No softness to this beauty.
Space tears open. A voice
shouts at him to wake. Flame

sears his heart with love and pain.
Its brevity is bittersweet relief.
Each morning of its flowering

the secretary passes on her way
to work, and stops –
an inhalation:

rose-tipped flare
in the desert of her day.
One weekend, in her absence,

Blake sells papers at the market,
scooped petals shed – their glow
replaced by soft, dissembling green.

Injury

Glass snaps, a shard drives hard
into his wincing foot. Then
stranded, too weak to stand,

too feverish to sleep, he sways,
hovers, rides the crest –
its burning tide laps his eyes,

inspires him to heat a small knife,
dig into his own flesh, prise out
the reddened chunk, thick gout

of blood. Glossy, wet.
Body lightens. He sighs.
This time there'll be no infection.

Now the lulls between his bouts –
aching sickness – seem to shrink,
to store up weakness for ascension.

His face now seems so small it almost
disappears. To himself he looks a ghost –
shade of some forgotten relative.

Once a week or so
she'll cross the river,
make the trip to see her sister.

Long, digressive caravan,
past two Shelters. Who
sleeps in either one?

Where does Blake sleep?
Survival makes him ill.
Lungs, veins. Even his eyes

are tainted, shamed.
He makes excuses for
his health as if she'll

think him spendthrift;
strains to talk –
to show cooperation

while preserving inner
distance. What should
he give for a dollar?

Dictation

She'll listen to the surgeon's voice,
squeezed small through foam-cupped disks.
Trace the pattern of his thoughts

through all his coughs and hesitations.
Sound-blocked bowl: outsiders
mouth or tap the glass –

press a switch to hear them.
Blake's more pressed.
The voice speaks through his ear,

flows down his arm, his pen,
pours onto paper. Sketching
now so fast, ecstatically, he moves

from transposition to collapse.
Falls sick – this sickness,
though, is music.

Blake drafts an angel for
an imaginary window. Fierce.
He works late. Gold

and orange for the robes,
he knows, but then
a bird flies through –

snaps the static frame. Wings
the same gold as the angel's
glow against an azure sky, cut by

flame. Towers burn. He works,
and works, his foot still aches;
its sole is hot and swollen.

I remember: I was young, walking
with my mother, hand-in-hand.
Or sailing on her shoulders.

When I was innocent, before I knew
this is where I could be. Shivering
green outside the liquor store, dying

in cruel boredom. Nothing but dull steps
towards survival. Nothing but a dream
of apple blossoms to sustain me.

Then I wandered down a laneway
with my mother – hedges sang
above our heads. Before I'd seen

angels but somehow knew
of them. Before I saw
that electrifying magnolia tree.

Casualties

Shock, for a child
who learns that "casualties"
aren't bruises (small

injuries, as implied
to a young etymologist)
but deaths: simple.

It takes longer
to conceive that we
might tell, screen

– before the birth
of cameras, paint
– yet not intervene

in war and damage.
Grown woman now,
she's learned to glide

by others, talk to Blake,
"feel his pain" as gurus
say – yet not –

A dollar, more, won't
do. And, if possible,
not desired. Like any

patient, Blake has pride.
Has learned with time
to wear his green

and yellow suffering
lightly. Only his eyes
– burn, flicker –

give him away. No,
of course, her heart won't break
for him. But it does ache.

Fever

The secretary's in a state.
Can't say what's come over her.
She frets at work, stays up at night –

something's near, she knows,
but what? The surgeon speaks
about his wife. Once again,

borders tremble. Photographs
of home, a golden puppy
in his arms. Naked, sexual.

Not the man she wants to see,
despite their half-pledged intimacy,
handmaiden and employer.

Drawn in to his story,
unwilling, while her own
lies out there floating

and eluding her. Somewhere,
also, Blake. Whose words
she dreams about, whose life

she almost knows. She
passes a half-open door, sees
a woman lying on the floor –

sees just her feet, in fact, then
other feet. Nurses, kneeling.
A tremor ripples through.

She walks by, continues
with her work. The fallen woman's
lifted, sent on for tests.

The Surgeon Stripped Down

Greens off. Clothes not yet on.
Small, compact, delicate spine.
Neat curve of a miniature paunch,

time's gift to discipline.
Ways to tell a man's profession
out of uniform. Athlete,

chef, engraver…their hands
need equal steadiness.
The surgeon's hands

are calloused, veined,
nails worn flat by work
and so much washing.

He's tired. Rubs eyes. Pressure
in his sinuses – winter, cold,
and for a moment

humanity's affliction:
– do animals know it? –
just beyond his skin,

lost, hovering. A blip.
Sudden fissure in the seam.
He dresses quickly: suit,

white coat, his armature.
Takes in the light, a colleague's face.
Back at his desk he asks

for messages, then lunch –
the same as yesterday – another trick
to re-establish balance.

Shit

He plunges deep
in their *places of love*
that are excrementitious,

deeper than anyone
who loves them.
Elegant men, angry children

learn what Timerman knows:
dignity need not
reside in self-control –

that's luck, not character,
no match for kindness.
Under the surgeon's hands flow

fluid, cud-like juices, from man-
made valves – almost sweet-
smelling – green and innocent.

Outside, on winter streets,
dog-shit, frozen, whorled,
ersatz cones and minarets

sit rigid on the pavement.
Once a year the surgeon makes
his own appointment,

the flexed, intelligent snake
noses his intestine, and
of this, he knows:

a brief surrender
saves life, makes him
more human, more humane.

Love and the Surgeon

What does he see
when he makes love? He
who knows the body

unpeeled, sectioned: muscle,
blood and coiled intestine.
Torn, inner smells smashed

open, made external,
cling to everything,
pour from and fill

all crevices. A novice
faints from this: bowel
unleashed, stomach contents,

organs, vivid, hot. Live
slaughter or the tannery:
vats of ochre and sienna,

brown and umber. Trouser-legs
and sleeves rolled up,
all stained with vivid dye.

Love, II

The surgeon's florist sends a bill,
one "presentation bouquet"
for his wife: her birthday

(and each anniversary). Small
window: the secretary sees
in the receipt's transparency

cold flowers arrive.
Veined, dark red and rubbery.
Is choice implicit in the order placed?

His wife knows he loves her
but still… does the cellophaned arrival
pall, ever? Same every year.

Evening

The tail end of the day. The sky
has squeezed itself slit-eyed –
a rim of pink. The rest is iris-indigo.

She's typed her schedules, put them
on the surgeon's desk. And he sits
thoughtful in his darkened office.

Perhaps replaying his five-hour surgeries –
two, side-by-side. He walks between
two rooms, two people's guts waiting

for his hands to touch and seal
them. Perhaps remembering
childhood, or his daughters' infancy.

He looks tired. His eyes are shadowed,
mimic sadness. She leaves him there
and goes out to the night. Flees

the hospital, the sleeping patients who,
fed a little stream of morphine now
at intervals, will wake repeatedly

this night, and see the surgeon
first thing in the morning, checking
on the aftermath.

Fatigue does often mimic sorrow –
almost is, at least its echo
in the body. Children know this.

Tiredness for them is premonition –
a day ends in tears, as often threatened.
Small, bitter sips of adult desolation

afflict a happy child, confirm
the prescience of a wise one.
Winter's early – snow and leaves

tossed together. Salt and salad,
ice and pepper. One vast cold supper.
More than in summer, this avenue is sunken,

magnolia's radiance now a dream.
When she was a child in another city,
this time of day was melancholy also,

but had the drawn-in warmth of stories.
The house was an ark on the sea of night,
the Babel of TV not yet a part of it.

What's this? Pastoral reverie?
Of course that time was no safer, only her
apprehension of its worries less complete.

At dusk, sometimes, as a child,
she was dressed up, eating supper, fed
a swift synopsis of the play she soon would see

and hear. Now underground and overhead
the city emits a muted roar, its overture.
Warming up. Blood under a stethoscope,

water on the shore. The sound of traffic:
travellers leave space emptied
in one place, fill it in another.

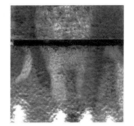

SAVING TIME

Daylight Savings Time

The secretary's favourite day:
she wins an extra hour.
All lost time flickers
and returns itself to her.

Skinnybones

Carved skeleton behind
the bars of a marble tomb
topped by a lovely, stylized form:

young woman. Calm, immaculate.
Small church, stagnant summer.
Heavy smell of sun-soaked grass.

Cold inside, slowly they creep
towards her, kneel and peek
at Skinnybones. Something squeaks.

They run breathless from
the churchyard, screaming.
Half-convinced the ghost

of Skinnybones is after them.
Her lesson has no sugar-coating.
No shadowy angels, sleep. Here

their physical end's laid out.
No cosy Sunday school
but rigorous, stiff-spined faith.

Death no tragedy, merely the end
of corporeal being. The reward,
the next full step.

The Park

Behind the Commonwealth Museum
an old stone house where tea is served.
Narrow benches and tame fields

where keepers watch the birds
and hippies, sniff the air
at rock concerts, later

pierce torn wrappers, hair
and sticky condoms
with their rusting spikes.

The edges of the park, a hostel.
Two men from a basement window
call her in. One's naked.

(She would have gone, but Magda
pulls her back.) Come in, come in.
He holds out his hand,

to lead her. A precipice,
a window ledge
she longs and fears to cross.

Always, Not Always

Always evening. Always fall
or early winter. Street lights burn;
soft discs smudge into brown

haze. Not always.
Sometimes, in the green
and white of spring

she sat with an old friend
in the park, where mint
made its own season,

cool summer; fragrant
warmth in winter's rain.
He told her of waking

to its smell, subtle blossoming
in tea. Of the fountain where
his daughter liked to play;

the plane's white wings, stains
on shuddering tarmac
where he trained younger men.

Back in the city where they talked
she wakes. Cut-glass
in a strange apartment shimmers

deep, obsessive blue,
fills her eye. In the air,
he told her, land, your loved ones

fall away so easily…. It's here,
now, you feel it, faces
turn dispassionate, eyes

glance off you, flicker with some
hostile feeling. But there,
you let it go, hands free.

Except in the whining surge
of take-off and descent
when the earth, its contents,

pull with such force
you beg them not
to let you leave.

The Day Is Held

The day is held at head and tail
by the hands of morning and evening –
stanzas when light changes its mind,

hours when her body releases.
This is it, the hour of peace –
if she had faith, this is when she would pray.

Every morning and each evening
part of the poem of the day.
Each a poem, each just a line,

each face, each building
syllabic. Dizziness-inducing:
all the work there is to do.

A job for a slew of poets
– and here: not three, not two,
but one, some days less than half a one.

Tower and Dome

Beside the CN Tower
– that unplunged hypodermic –
a bubble of thin air.

Off-season carnival, dull sun.
So warm. How can it be November?
Planet Hollywood's still packed

with visitors. Theatre-goers
stream to dinner. On Queen,
kids preen by City TV.

Up and down, hot oil
jumping in a pan.
 "Pick me, pick me!"

Skip two months. Clouds so low,
the Dome's a sulking shoulder
hunched against its head, the Tower.

Ridged, unimposing stalk
half-visible. Lights cast grainy flares
in mist, scummy pools

of slush at each street corner. Cars
spread icy ruffles when they turn,
pedestrians jump back as if they'll burn, not freeze.

Snow

Blake dreams himself alone,
standing on a stone shore.
Then with his mother,

– hand-in-hand his younger brother.
Both boys pulled from sleep,
they walk and walk. Snow burns.

Soon unshod feet, bare hands
wear shrouds of absent feeling,
gloved and slippered numbness.

Figures on pyjamas disappear,
snow-flocked, a white shawl
covers hair, slides down,

clouding necks and shoulders.
Blake doesn't drop his brother's hand.
They reach the bus station, mama

determined to go – where? "Away from here."
A cop who stepped inside to cheat the cold
will stop them. Eyes alert with questions.

Nativity Photograph

Is that him? Dour-faced
in strap-on wings, shoulders
braced, wire halo slipping.

Gravity sits hard on this choir's
sweating chorus, each child
an emblem of absorption – St. George's

congregation, called "urban,"
means "immigrant." Saturdays
they stand in line

at Harrison Baths, wait for
hot water. Eyes closed
in the steam sometimes Blake

can see the crowded valley,
his brother (taken in
by an uncle's family),

and somewhere zeroed
among hospital accounting
his mother, freed from them.

Blake's Aunt Unguarded

She sits at table, resting,
chin in hands. If
he had a photograph

it would be this: dusk,
or later. Coat off, or on.
Face undefended, young

and old. Bridge and temples
stained rose, marked by frames.
Outside this frame she'll stand,

light the stove or finish chores
left over. Ask to see his work,
to hear the choir's new song.

Salvage

The bitter smell of winter
underground. Trains
with wooden floors,

sweat-dyed leather.
This is later, will be
for the secretary, filed

under nostalgia. Now
in the ruins of St. George
snow and ash dance, turn air

the grainy black-and-white
of underwater wrecks
thick-mossed with silt.

The only colour shards of glass
that shattered late last night
with high explosive music.

Men pick through the ruins,
Blake with them. He stops,
his boot meets softness

heavier than snow. Ragged
shapes tucked low beneath
a fallen beam. Five kittens,

new fur spiked with soot
and frost. Their mother
licks Blake's foot, eats salt

from its cold rim, tries
seducing his attention
from her babies. "Leave her,"

says the minister. "They're safe
for now. Let them shelter
with the birds." Blake's eyes fly

the arc of a gloved hand to see
where hunched birds claim unroofed
pillars: scorched, impromptu trees.

Blake at the Clinic

"Breathe in." Cold. "Hold it."
Breath suspends, takes flight
upward, angelward. Colder.

"Breathe out." Faintness
grips him. He steps out to
a whisky-filtered sky.

Years since that taste
has seared his tongue. Now
its warmth might ease

the leaden squeeze
around his lungs, scour
his head of memories.

X-Ray

Late. The technician rubs his arms
against the chill, Siberian.
Bronchial trees stunted

and abandoned, landscape
starved and over-used.
The Aral Sea is two-thirds dust,

and no-one, least of all
himself, wants to walk
Blake's wilderness.

Blake in Union Station

Horribly lucid.
Terribly awake to pain.
Hungry, he wanders

through Union Station.
Hears the unisexual voice
announce the in and out of trains.

The flickering leaves of the timetable –
white hovers on black: delay, arrival.
Everyone caught up in industry,

everyone but Blake, who's come
to sit, escape the cold and
steel himself for more.

Another bout with winter,
with eyeless faces – or at least
whose eyes are turned away from him.

St. George the Martyr

She wants to disappear
to the space at the back
of the library stacks,

a courtyard in Prague, the garden
of St. George the Martyr
where gulls cut through the air,

soft speech lulls her ear,
prickles of warm languor
raise the small hairs on her arms.

A trance-like peace. Clear
sight of the evening sky,
crystalline. The bird

still beats its golden wings.
In the sea-shell quiet of the garden
tired martyrs sleep.

AGE AND THE SECRETARY

Film Sets

She loathes the film-crews –
self-important, bottom-
heavy gait, all cell-phones

and free doughnuts.
Their ramps and cables
make her late. They stare

through passers-by. And
their interference shrinks
the borders of the sky.

Still, they do provide diversion.
She's seen Jon Voight,
and that Canadian actor

– what's his name –
and one long day,
on break, she watched

a "stakeout" on the roof
of Sick Kids hospital resolve
with gunfire after several takes.

Fire Drill

All elevators stop.
A minute, then the stairwells
are echo chambers, concert halls

sprayed with gunshot coughs.
Laughter, running – any break
in dry routine is warm oil

easing the machinery of the day.
A little click, whir, restart,
purring now, no longer groaning.

The Secretary's Nephew

A tight, fat bud – his face – opens,
unclenching from the moment
of his birth, unfolding

to the air, to life.
Such sweetness there! A bee
might land and suck the honey

of his breath, its infant sweetness.
His birth, like Blake's memory,
another country far away,

shadows her imagination.
The baby's essence reaches her
in smooth packets, each few months.

Each glossy slip a record
of his growth. His little face
becomes a flower, his mouth the bud

as his whole being fans outward;
he begins the journey too. She hoards this
photograph, won't put it up at work

as the others do – too precious.
They won't feel this pulse,
this heat, when they look at him,

so she keeps him in her purse,
holds him in her hand
to watch him sleeping.

Night baby, child of night. Secrets
in his head don't yet exist.
Eyes sealed behind

tiny pouches; small, broad nose.
Top lip a bird's wing, a soft
chapeau, so delicately tented.

In another picture, open-eyed,
he points, inclining, to the sun: his mother.
Milk-smears glisten on his tongue.

Little bumps on his brow
where satin brows will grow.
Dark hair, sea-moss on his skull.

Night baby, child of night
is what his name means – and he lives
most completely in her dreams

where she smiles and sings him lullabies.
As the night belongs to him
he need never fear it.

This she wishes for him, since night
has always nursed her deepest dread.
Just as she begins to sink towards

sleep her body balks;
pulls back from blindness,
death's approximation.

Age and the Secretary

The secretary feels age
ticking through her bones.
Flesh slips, self blurs at the edges.

The agonizing creep of time
marked by the computer's clock.
Panic, guilt, at wishing

so much time away. One day
at the gift shop, she says
to a bronze-armed volunteer –

a gilded, crystal-haired
survivor, forearm blued
with a forced tattoo –

"Thank god tomorrow's
Friday." A rigid hand grips
the secretary's wrist.

Missing her age by 10 years at least,
the volunteer says urgently: "Don't wish
your whole young life away."

And truly, the secretary tries
to follow this advice, but resolve
evaporates before ennui,

and then, the flu:
in the washroom
where the secretary rests

her burning head against
the stall, one woman
tells another of god's love

for her. But as the listener
begins, blossoming, to nod,
agree, and voice her own epiphany,

god's messenger moves on to flatter
new conference attendees.
God's love indeed! The secretary

shakes with fever and disgust,
the second heightened by the first –
she feels its echo in her wrist.

A Daughter

Two friends; one day-old
daughter. Stunned by her presence,
its dark, ripe scent. Pores infused

by sweetness, breath thick
from lack of sleep and too much coffee,
dry from cigarettes unsmoked.

A simple fact, necessity.
The birth turned difficult,
ended in C-section. The baby

lifted out straight into light.
The secretary's friend, fright
now softened into pain,

sleeps in and out
(a cradle of drugs),
wakes to her daughter.

The Secretary on Holiday

Jet lag in a strange city. Waiting
for a room, and for her lover
to arrive – he's coming from Slovakia –

the secretary wanders Wenceslas Square,
whose air is shimmering with
the dissipated haze of her fatigue.

She feels drunk. Faces elongate,
or widen, then recede. Smoke
from coffee hovers, ebony

droplets rise and damp her hair.
Small change hits a saucer
like the arrival of a train.

Groups of travellers cluster, armed
with maps. Dependent, thrown together,
pairs walk hand-in-hand,

their footsteps shortened, smaller.
She floats for now, but soon
she'll join the tourist kindergarten.

Vysehrad. Here a beautiful,
bare-breasted woman
commemorates the death

of a small, bald man. Or so
the secretary imagines him. By now,
her dreams have emptied of

the ringing phone embedded
in the surgeon's desk. Just the former shadow
of the phone exists...an aureole that echoes.

The secretary and her lover
take their own childish steps together,
walk dazed through streets

whose air is clouded by the maze
of mysterious construction
inside hidden courtyards.

Green leaves turn pale with dust,
ferns wilt beneath its accumulated weight.
This is a dream now, will be more so later,

the secretary knows. The song
that haunts her in Toronto
even stronger here in Prague.

Its minor key, of course,
melancholy. Strange comedy
of camouflage; evasion.

The rain it raineth ev'ry day.
It rains, and rains –
not in Prague, but later in Berlin,

where regiments of cranes
are swung from side to side
by rain-swept wind.

Berlin

A crane protrudes beyond the darkened hill,
extending like a military arm
into an evening sky whose air has paled
under the rust of a dissolving sun.
This summer, each horizon of the city
thickens with chorus-lines of bristling cranes,
each arm a token for some hundred men
shipped in to hasten the restructuring.
They sleep in boxy trailers, bunked in fours
or more, their visas only good this year.
One face, reclining on its owner's side,
bright-eyed with homesickness, observes them pass.
They've just come from the ruins of the Wall
and hurry by, towards a warm hotel.

The Painting

Child sits under carved stone
bench, on which lies prone,
face-down, a marble man.

The room is smeared with light,
and on the wall, indented, small
translucent heads, recessed.

The child sucks his thumb.
Having seen a reproduction
years before, she knew the scene

as funeral parlour, boy crouched
beneath his father's coffin.
The light was different, too.

Bridges

The secretary returns to Prague, alone –
this time just as the summer heat unwinds
itself from heavy skies to wrap her heels

and ankles in its tendrils, climb her thighs,
encircle her unyielding waist – whose inner
walls are still rose-stained with radiant dye,

a maze of broken passages, locked doors –
and draw her to green shade above the city.
She climbs the hill to Vysehrad, from where

she likes to watch the shining river
tremble in its sleeve below. The dead
at Vysehrad spin out their lures beyond

the gates, along the paths that fan towards
a statue skirted by an iron fence.
They beckon visitors inside their home

whose streets are overhung with ferns and leaves,
whose covered walks, ceilinged with stars and moons,
small butterflies, drip gold striations, glow

with frosted grapes, scrolled ironwork,
– all the accessories of paradise.
Her favourite tomb is guarded by a woman,

half-naked, lower body draped, arms raised
behind her head as women do, as she
herself has done, to flatter her own breasts

for someone else. (When this occurs in films
she yawns and looks away.) This afternoon
the sun adorns the statue's hips, adds scarves

of light to her stone draperies, prints leaves
across the slab behind her head. Is she
seducing or protecting? Now it's time

to go. The secretary starts to climb
the stairway down from hill-top to the river –
she stops, looks down upon the water,

a man and woman arguing below,
absorbed in their own youthful drama,
playing a scene for anyone who cares

to look. She sees the nether parts of homes,
their private sides exposed. Their balconies
unshuttered, bedrooms open to her eyes.

Inside one, a desk with papers lifted
by the breeze. A row of red slate roofs.
Lower, the river, rumpled silk, its sheen

rubbed off, is creased, unrolled, then ironed smooth
again. Small boats and tourist barges sew
a seam along its surface, underneath

the bridges. Bracelets echo in a series:
brick, iron, stone. Confining air and light,
they bind two halves, soar over islands where

the cafés have the same names as before
the thaw, same patrons. Exiles have returned
to claim their favourite seats, teach their children

how to live with more history, less space.
How does a city know its own transformed
existence? Recent past becomes old news,

and those with longer memories must now
welcome oblivion, find storage space,
renovate their old imaginations.

The Airport

Sharp smell of terminals:
currency, engine oil,
brand-new luggage,

perfume slips that fall
from magazines. Liquor,
snack food, dry-cleaned

uniforms – mixed scent of travel.
Walk through the gates alone.
Yawning hallways, lounge,

inner waiting room. Then
the earth's last junction:
thin sleeve from wall

to plane. Wind
and engines press its sides.
Sensible, it shudders.

CLINIC DAY

Clinic Day

On the ledge today, the circus.
Observe the secretaries
in their natural habitat –

that is to say,
captivity. Regard
their furtive eating style,

crouched behind their desks.
Speared by a dozen pairs
of eyes. True captives: patients.

The Other Secretary

The other secretary's dreams are filled
with ringing phones. Names and voices
she can't now decipher, old language.

The school she knew, the hospital
she worked at, gone. House, orchard.
Her husband blames her parents

for the loss. Split by trees and rotting cherries,
family divides, two sides. Some friends wait,
others walk the roads. Phones are dead except

at night, in sleep. The room's so hot. Across
the bed her political opponent sweats.
The phone does ring: an invitation. Join us

next week. Storm the embassy. Lost
at work, she spends each night in fruitless search:
rumour, static. Who rakes up the dark-brown clot?

Number Twenty-Three

Surgeon number twenty-three
in the list, alphabetically,
an old-fashioned rogue, outdated.

Lecherous, wholly self-inflated,
mocked by secretaries for
his graceless sexual repartee,

even he surprises her.
On her morning pee-break
beside the room where he performs

minor but still painful work
under local anaesthetic
she hears him calm a frightened man.

"Don't worry! Relax!" shouts Dr. R.,
(he's slightly deaf), avuncular,
then starts an ersatz *Oklahoma!*

Captivated, she sits, unseen,
longer than necessary or wise
(cold porcelain, remember); ignores

the draft around her thighs,
while next door, Dr. R. exhorts:
"Come on, come on!" *"You're doin' fine…."*

The Surgeon-in-Chief

The surgeon-in-chief
likes to sit in the dark.
His antidote to trauma.

From the O.R.'s noisy heat
to his meditation garden.
Opaque waters, pale

fins shimmer grey.
The crackle of an X-ray
breaks the peace, light snaps on.

His Feet

Little gel-pearls shiver
in curvy soles
of wondrous running shoes.

When he walks, his tendons
tighten on the stair-ledge –
one flight from office

to O.R., easy in his *airsoles*.
Watch that little bubble rise,
tremble with his body.

His Reputation

He can claim the world
a civilized, respectful place
whose people, almost

everywhere he goes,
are predisposed to honour him,
their guest, their expert.

Rarely overlooked, seldom
offered insult; the slights
that might occur if

he rode the subway or
like his colleague down the hall
shopped furtively for lingerie.

New Math

Souls loosen after hours. We all know that.
The secretary helps the surgeon
order slides for next day's lecture, and

as light subsides, he talks. Slow,
subliminal, his words. On privacy,
worn by his parents to prevent

disinterment. The silence
in his house that held him from
his mother's past. His feeling

that concealment had made havoc
in her cells – he shrugs. *Who knows?*
At last, though, he's revealed,

a little, to the secretary: shorn
of memory, he's inspired to dig; uncoil
the body's deepest histories; keep

secrets; wear, in adulthood,
a child's clear stare. Later, alone
she stares herself at photographs,

tries to make them open.
His mother, small, like him,
less aging than receding, self-

contained, smile fenced in
by deep brackets, one for each
dead child. The secretary tries

and fails to read her face, to pierce
her sleeve to blue – the hidden digits
old math: subtraction, long division.

EXCAVATE

The Wall Opens

Stare at the surface: wall,
its shadowed corners.
Windows, desk.

Spines of unread books,
carpet patterns, clothes
thrown over chair-backs.

The same framed view. Stare
and stare, wait for dissolution,
for something to break open.

The Bird

Morning: the promise
of false dawn. She looks up
from the streetcar window

where her elbow rests.
A bird beats its wings – flash of red
then gold against a vivid sky.

Clear as the heightened edge
of drunkenness – before all edges blur
and nothing's clear.

The bird beats its golden wings,
symbol of day's offerings –
by night, flown.

Nothing spectacular, this loss.
Just the trace of separation
from her self for so much time

in any day. The natural state of all
who work in institutions; small
reprieves are pools in time,

oases out of place.
She blinks, and when
she looks again the sun

has moved. The bird's
a pigeon, brown, the sky
a dull November blue.

Excavate

Old City Hall: leafless trees
sleeved in pinprick lights –
radiant winter flowers.

On Queen Street
ghost-signs flare,
shadowing the new.

The drop-in centre used to be
a bank – CIBC –
cash-slot fused by fire.

Tonight the secretary shivers,
snow displaces dust,
a dark sky glitters.

On holiday, the surgeon
rents a small plane,
floats on air. Below –

the pilot shows –
a medieval village rises,
grassy bumps and furrows

where houses, laneways,
sewers used to be.
Earthed over, now

seen from above:
bodies, clothed and turning,
press shallow surface.

Severance

Two sooty Xs smudged on brick.
A sign stuck to the window:
Closed For Renovations.
On the door, non sequitur:
Why Did U Fire Me Bitch?

High Finance

On King Street Blake looks up at towers
in wonder, head tilted back.
(The wind, for once gentle, declines

to attack; to whip through the street
in hurtling volleys. An aureole, professorial
of grey hair lifts around his head.)

Lost, overcome,
he's a shrunken squirrel,
dwindling flesh to burgeoning gloss.

Their luminous hardness is wild,
not civilized. They need him as little
as trees do, though he built them,

has cleaned them. Powered at night
they send glowing ladders of light up the sky.
Take over the air, set off its beauty,

ignore it and him completely.
Around them the sky's a mauve blur,
an icy cocktail, shaken, not stirred.

Clouds float, frail lemon twists
spiralling through mirrored glass.
This is a shell, dissected to see through:

one side of the world to the other.
Rock, lava, fathomable water.
The streets are deep channels,

waiting to flood. Skateboarders ride
the low currents at night, loving
the avenues for their utility. Fearless

surfers, these tatty marauders
still prefer one shabby ski
to the smooth ergonomics of shark-sleek blades.

They rocket past the lost sky-watcher.
He holds his breath – one boy in particular
will shoot into an oncoming tour bus

– silver cylinder filled with blind heads.
The boy falters, floats, turns his board,
and skids just short of the crashing tide.

Subway Music

A young boy, leaning,
rhythm pounding in his head.
The perfect manufactured cover –

not a sneer, exactly, but a stare,
a wall of cool, mechanical,
hinged tight on minimalist doors.

Hips move to the music, all
movement small, controlled.
Blake can hear the tiny spray

of sound, threaded by
the trumpet's silver scream.
Puncturing thought

it teases, hints. Remember?
No, that's not it.
Next to him a girl, hypnotized

by rap, two ears bookends,
sandwiching the beat.
Sound leaks out from either side –

on one, dull bass,
the other full, didactic voice.
Jewelled noise, studded

sound, and not one
undefended moment.
No eye contact with anyone

outside the code.
Not with each other. Not with him.
Sealed from the light, the night, the fray.

Mice

Soot-backed, supple travellers
dart soft as water, thread
the subway's mercury,

brush feet in dark theatres:
swift hair-pricking shudders.
Stoic and forlorn,

these shrunken foragers,
blind and deaf from darkness,
the train's hot rush,

burnt from skimming rails.
Their cousins, squirrels,
furred gargoyles, freeze

stiff-legged when she passes.
Sniff grass, stitch it with crossings,
small hustlers, teeth bared.

The Bear

Dream of the Bear: an Inuit
drawing on the wall. Or is it
Scream of the Bear? The secretary,
passing, mimes her own bare scream.

Bridges II

The railway bridge, its arch inelegant
and soot-stained, scoops a hollow from the snow.
She hears her feet take muffled bites of crispness,

small breaths escape her lungs like birds set free
from open hatches; fly towards the necks
of connoisseurs discussing blow-jobs.

"I love it when she takes both balls inside
her mouth" one says. The secretary sees
the grimy seam in too-tight jeans and dreams:

soft pearls inside a wrinkled chamois sack,
rubbed smooth by pressure, musky-scented, damp.
The winter light is harsh and blued by cold,

a light that seeps through blinds, emblazons scars
with whiteness, filters ice inside. It waits
beyond the edges of the bed. That's home.

Another Wanderer

Sometimes this city tests her heart.
And should. She walks home
from an early Christmas party.

A man adrift at Bathurst Street
and Bloor accepts her money.
"How are you?" Face screwed up –

a child's – his words a child's, too:
"I want to go home." Home tonight
or home forever? Most likely: home never.

Constantinople

Years before, the secretary
leaves her job, gives up her room,
departs a ruined love affair,

returns to England, once her home.
Walks through London in a trance,
fixing on these random sights:

El Greco's painting, black and silver
storm that causes her to shudder;
pair of yellow shoes for sale;

scarred statue in a park
whose gravel walks lead into
memory, too. From London through

a bleak sequence: off-season
beaches, St. Malo (putty-grey);
vacant hostels, icy-floored;

abandoned Alpine villages;
volcanic islands in the south
whose fine black sands scald naked feet.

There she meets another woman,
outrunning her own bitter weather
(snow all the way to Buffalo

where no-one in the clinic
knew her. Boyfriend quiet
the long drive home

turns quieter still, stops calling.
Two months later, hunkered
at the cash in Birk's: him. "Hey Babe."

He's buying an engagement ring.)
The secretary and her friend
arrive in Istanbul. Walk through

the gardens, grey and olive-green;
eat scented nuts that stain their lips
and fingers; stand at night before

the river, marvel at the old city.
They meet a man who's travelling
with two small sons. The boys are tanned,

hair blanched by sun. Men stop them
in the street, touch their white heads,
caress their faces, give them sweets.

One day the women go to a *hamam*.
The building's old, of course, stone walls
made still more beautiful by stains.

Wild birds fly past the roof.
The secretary and her friend the only visitors,
wear plastic sandals, shed their clothes

behind them in the antechamber.
A bare-breasted woman leads them
through long, steam-obscured rooms.

Water sluicing down from spouts
fills wide stone bowls. First hot: she scrubs
and scours them – dirty children – 'til

their skins ache. Then cold: they lie still,
gaping, fish-like on the tiles. They rise,
pay the attendant, start to dress. She smiles

at the secretary's friend, flicks one breast,
gently. "You: madame." Turns to
the secretary. "You: mademoiselle."

The New Roof

The house is full of foreign sound.
Its roof half off reminds her
of Berlin's Hollow Tooth:

ruined, sheared and soaring.
First the wind, its sea-borne voice
as the tarp's throaty sail

swallows and exhales.
Wet noise that's also dry:
the crackling of rain.

The house a vessel, now,
sailing where? This,
the loneliest, harshest weather,

short of winter – for the homeless
traveller. Against his will an odyssey
whose end is yet more open sea.

The Sleeping Knight

A ruby-headed bird observes
the sleeper, still as a knight in his tomb,
arms in the formal position of prayer.

The grass collects dew.
His skeleton's not far removed,
it sleeps beneath his skin and,

in repose, it almost wins.
His cheeks are stark, their greyness
armours him. His clothes a mesh

of chains, tattoos and scarves torn,
shredded and retied – a motley camouflage.
The dog beside him guards his piece

of hard-earned sanctuary.
Night cloaks their limbs
in grey tranquility.

The Resident On Call

Hates this frozen cubicle.
Tense and chafing in his clothes
he dreads the gritty, feverish thrill

of being dragged from stupor
to confront whatever trauma
washes in. To fake compassion

in the midst of need to sleep
so deep his organs ache.
He sees pneumonia, lots of it.

Strange outbreaks of Bell's palsy.
And the continuous brigade
of scarecrows – some Samaritan

will always make the call –
who stink, and drink, beg for drugs.
One or two, though dazed, half-human.

And still T.B. Headless horseman,
undead, cantering again,
even colleagues thrown ashore

on Mantoux island.
Before this, but post-Mann,
only the poor afflicted,

now scores of landed immigrants
from Serbia or China
have brought it home.

The waiting room's an airport lounge –
slung between events,
no matter their anxiety,

those who sit there pilgrims, briefly free
from any task except to wait.
Oh Christ! (His pager calls.)

Balance

For every pain or pleasure, there
will be its compensation –
its equal, opposite reaction

that may skip a generation.
She watches as Blake sleeps.
Breathing tube taped to his nose,

he whistles, long-beaked bird,
restless in drugged repose.
Later, she makes love, each burst

of pleasure mirroring
his pain – no! Clamp shut
the valves of extra-sensory feeling.

Night Gardens

If memory's lyric,
science is logic
scanning ruins

while memory puns.
The past ticks, preserved
in cells, spasmodic.

Night gardens push
through sleep-wires.
Blake's dreams,

morphine-wrapped,
green, morph red. Moths.
A cloud, rising

where the church roof
once held together
song and prayers.

The sky, squared, opens
in the half-light.
Garden unwalled,

image tunnelled
small. Here, a bed.
He sleeps, rafting time.

Fertility Test

Seeding grit, her body
forks itself above air.
He who examined her –

fed her Lethe's waters,
brought her back – now tells her,
in a room that smells of bleach:

internal scars build up,
adhesions make soft tubes
impassable. *See here*: she reads

the lab report. Stage right,
a residential chorus, following
the same map, nods accord.

"There is a surgical procedure,
sometimes, but…" he looks at her.
"In your case, not…."

A well-trimmed door
falls shut, its soft thud
barely audible.

Inside Furama Cakes
a low, internal hum.
Stopped car on a wet street,

windows slowly fogging.
Light, buttery and sweet.
She sits quiet, self-soothing

as her nephew does
to lull himself to sleep.
Hot spots, damage, lit

by one glowing eye.
An inner map
all cul-de-sacs,

blocked lanes and
permanently barred roads.
Well, now she knows.

The Secretary's Eye

The secretary has lapses.
Instances of blindness when
she misses what's most vital.

At the age of six...no seven,
a speck of glass pierced her routine.
Mysterious chance: a tiny grain

found the near-centre of her eye –
unnoticed, might have stayed, but she
was being taught calligraphy.

Her copy books revealed
a crazy swooping graph –
stock-market, boom to crash –

instead of the usual regiment
of curling, ornamental script.
When the teacher asked

about a cognitive impairment,
the secretary's mother was incensed.
"My child could read at four!"

she cried – but later,
over coffee, scrutinised
her daughter's efforts. Chaos.

Science invoked. The little secretary
trots with her mother to the doctor,
errant eyes are bathed in belladonna

then examined. "Something there, no
question," says the ocular inspector, so...
body sleeps, surgery's performed,

another body, foreign – glass – excised.
This marks a brief but influential chapter
in her childhood since, on waking from

the operation (medically successful)
to an empty room, she finds herself,
unwarned and unattended, blind.

A child with well-fed imaginative powers,
she had, as her mother said, begun to read
quite young, and knows her share

of horror tales – has woken to one now.
She lies quiet for a minute; panic
flutters, flaps its wings, fans

a slow explosion from her throat,
first dry, post-anaesthetic croak
then mounting, childish howl.

A nurse arrives, tries to calm her.
Hands, felt by the unseeing child
to be malevolent and wild,

advancing to the thrashing head
to soothe, instead are bitten.
Now the nurse howls, mother

rushes in, then doctor – apologies
and explanations: "normal side-effect,
wears off, careless omission," etc.

"All's well, piece of glass, god
knows how it got there, but removed.
Tiny scar, will fade then disappear…."

All that's left: a jewelled streak
on ovoid white, a ruby chip. Scar,
in contradiction to the doctor's thesis

stays and grows, embedded in
the secretary's eye as those
blind moments fasten to her memory.

Flesh, Paper

A man dying, a newborn
sleeping put hard labour
in. Sustenance: breath

comes fast in its rotations,
eyes quiver under lids.
At the hospital's back door,

garbage lane: lime rivers flow
from hot containers, full-blown
exhalations. Rot and flowers.

Inside the wards, conditioned
to repel the muggy air, Blake's room.
By fluke, all beds but his are empty.

She sits beside him, shimmying
the metal rung beneath him.
Restless foot-taps. Silver

shuttle: here to there.
Blake sleeps, or hides.
The rapid cycling of his heart

like water turned high
on a stove, boiling dry.
A locker holds his clothes,

a stash of papers. News clippings
from the fire, fifty years ago. Photo:
him, a boy, standing in the choir.

Phone numbers, nameless. Half-done
sketches for engravings no-one's seen.
In the secretary's bag a letter

waits. She'll read it later
in St. George's garden. Reach
out. One finger on Blake's wrist –

too heavy, too intrusive. Pull back.
How long will he last? Can blood
renew once more, or

is this it? Where is he now?
Back entrance: nostrils clench against
the heat. A woman drops the butt-end

of her cigarette, steps back
behind revolving glass that shows
the secretary her own face, circling.

Smoke leaks up and sideways,
skips, a fragile wave. From flesh,
paper, wet-tipped, drying

in the breeze. One moment
held inside a shining lip,
the next burned out.

What Opens?

Light flashing
through the filigree
of garden hedge.

A woman alone
on a far bench.
A bird in motion

frozen, white on blue.
Expectation or
nostalgia warps

the meaning
of these gaps.
Let them open.

B.C.

She walks one evening down a laneway
in the molten summer light. Each side,
leaves tremble: faces flare

like candle flames as they approach.
Trees wait, hold arms out in suspension.
The road's a furrow: dark through dusk.

Mosquitoes: clouds of smoke. Bodies
are submerged in light, hair caught
by sun's last flames: the wings of angels.

Air Mail

The grey cat dances,
pawing insects in the heat;
chasing one white butterfly,

rears up on strong hind legs.
Sprinklers rain on grass.
Teenagers sleep. The air hardly moves.

Dropped from the blue: "I got
your address from…" it starts,
and then: elusive details shiver.

Flight, wide road
to the airport. Sofa, where
the letter-writer sits at night.

"I know you as a friend," she writes.
My father told me how you met,
the garden where you sat and talked.

Please accept these, his
photograph and mine. Do let me know
if you receive them…. signed…."

a girl, and here's a boy at church, his wings
intact. Blake's history, once held fast
by him, now passed on by his daughter.

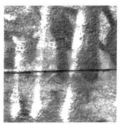

EPILOGUE

City Haiku

(with apologies to Paul Muldoon)

The pump flushes trash:
stones, leaves, traces of urine
expelled in the wash.

Two solitudes meet
or don't. Dogs and shit compete
for grass with tai chi.

You bring the coffee.
I'll save the thin-slatted bench
with most shade. Meet me.

Left on the church step:
broken shoe, plastic daisy
stuck to its pink strap.

Gunmetal, concrete:
The scarred, blunt head of a fish
bursts up from the street.

A flat-bed's gleaming
cargo: new toilets, shell-white
under rain streaming.

The sun moves higher.
Buildings flame: each floor a rung
of electric fire.

An ice-bitten breath.
The albino squirrel's tail
stiff as a white wreath.

Sunshine, half-cool air.
Winter drawing up behind
the clouds. Please, no more.

Starbucks: the new church.
Coffee, confession, penance
one warm ambience.

Silver flutes jut up
above. A roof organ or
ventilation pipes.

Wind after sundown.
River water turns over,
green folds into brown.

A peeled lichee sits.
The planetarium, veined
moon dropped from its nest.

3 a.m. Awake.
Suffering no more or less
for being godless.

Acknowledgements

Earlier versions of some of these poems were published in:
Alphabet City, *The Drunken Boat* (*www.thedrunkenboat.com*),
Grain, *The Literary Review of Canada*, *The New Quarterly*, and
SHORTFUSE: The Global Anthology of New Fusion Poetry,
eds. Todd Swift and Phil Norton, Rattapallax Press.

Thank you to Susan Olding and Margaret Christakos for
their generous contributions to this manuscript, and to John
Knechtel for his photographs. My deepest thanks to Ann Shin
for the twin gifts of her time and pitch-perfect readings of
these poems, and to my editor, Gary Draper, for his skill and
patience. And for their inspiration: Mire, Callum, Ayaan, Euan
and Geedi.

I would like to acknowledge the support of the Toronto Arts
Council and the Ontario Arts Council.

Diana Fitzgerald Bryden is the author of one other book of poetry, *Learning Russian*. Her poems have appeared in various publications and anthologies in Canada and the United States. She lives in Toronto and is currently working on a novel, *Mealtime*.